CONGREGATIONAL
FAVOR

Living Your Best Life
through Church Membership

Dr. Bryant K. Bell, Th.D.

Empowered Faith International
P. O. Box 156
Marietta, GA 30061
www.empoweredfaith.org

Congregational Favor
Living Your Best Life Through Church Membership
by Dr. Bryant K. Bell, Th.D.

ISBN 978-0-9768416-2-3

© 2012 Bryant K. Bell
Empowered Faith International
Marietta, Georgia 30061

For more information about Empowered Faith International, Enlightened Christian Center, call
770/218-6215 or visit www.empoweredfaith.org

Edited by Stanley Love. stanleylove@mail.com

Dedication

I dedicate this book to my wife's grandmother Mrs. Rosalie Woodall. For 60 years you have been faithful to your church in every way.

Acknowledgements

I give the greatest thanks to Jesus Christ, my Lord and Savior. Your grace and favor have enabled me to do more that I ever dreamed possible. I am forever grateful to you. Thank you to LySandra, my wife. You have been there with me to help build our lives, family and church. You still inspire me to achieve all that God has called me to do. Thank you to my children, Bryandra, Jeremy and Micaiah. Each of you, in your individual and unique ways, helps me to remain focused, young and strong. Thank you to Dr. Crelfo and Pastor Taffi Dollar. You are both solid role-models for me and my family to follow in Christ. Thank you for being our Spiritual Father and Mother and selflessly providing the resources and impartation for us to succeed. LySandra and I hope this book makes you both proud. Thank you to Bishop Kenneth Fuller. I have called you many times when I needed advice on church issues. Your advice always works. Thank you for being a great man of God who understands the needs of Pastors. Thank you to Stanley Love. You have been a great inspiration for this latest book. You have been a prize member, a great leader in our church, and a good editor for all of my books.

Contents

What is Congregational Favor?

. . . .

God loves His people. His acts of love toward us are limitless and boundless. One way which He expresses His love is through His loving favor. One way to define favor is God's ability, as the supreme ruler of all Heaven and Earth, used on our behalf, to benefit us in every way possible. When Jesus turned water into wine, He was using His supreme authority over earth's elements and heaven's miracles to benefit the wedding guests. Favor is God's Loving-kindness towards us.

Congregational Favor is the favor we receive when we join, attend, participate and defend our church. It is exclusive. It does not apply to all the people in the world nor does it apply to every Christian. It only applies to "church members". In order to experience Congregational Favor, you must be a member of a church. It doesn't have anything to do with how much you pray, how much you read the Word of God or how cute you are. Congregational Favor is reserved for those who are members of a church.

GOD HAS ALWAYS WANTED A CONGREGATION

God has always wanted a congregation to love and pour His favor upon. Contrary to the opinions of some, God loves His churches. This love includes the buildings and the people. He is into the "brick and mortar" and the "four walls." He loves them partly because they house His people and give Him a physical location in the communities of the world. Since God loves churches, we too should love his churches... all of them.

God's love for church is the basis for favor. It is the very essence of Congregational Favor. In Leviticus 26:11-12 he reveals His passion to love a group of people as church members by saying, *"And I will set my tabernacle among you: and my soul shall not abhor you. And I will walk among you, and will be your God, and ye shall be my people."*

Through the pages of this book, I want to introduce you to one way to walk in favor for the rest of your life. That favor comes as a result of being an active member of a local church.

Chapter 1

The Benefits of Joining a Church

One of the greatest decisions you will ever make is the decision to join a church. So many people have problems making this decision. They make decisions that have far greater negative consequences everyday and still cannot make a decision to join a church. People purchase cars, houses and boats on the whim but cannot make a decision to join a church. People go on dates with people they just met, have one night stands and even elope but cannot make a decision to join a church. People open credit lines, bank accounts and risky investments but cannot make a decision to join a church.

After salvation, joining a church is a decision that will produce some of the most positive rewards you will ever experience in life, yet so many people never experience these rewards. This is because the devil wants to destroy the children of God. He knows that Jesus loves the church and has provided great blessings for those who make a quality decision to join. There are several benefits of favor that you receive when you join a local church. Let's take a look a those benefits.

1. JOINING A CHURCH GIVES YOU ACCESS TO FAVOR IN THE SIGHT OF GOD

> But now hath God set the members every one of them in the body, **as it hath pleased him.** 1 Corinthians 12:18. [Emphasis added]

God sets every Christian in the church that He is pleased with them joining. Therefore, there is a church for every Christian. There is no reason why any person should say they cannot find a church. The reality is the devil does not want Christians to have a church because he knows the benefits they will experience when they join.

God assigns churches so you can be blessed and have the necessary teaching and training to fulfill the destiny that God has for your life. Notice the scripture says, "*as it hath pleased him.*" When God is pleased, it means that He is happy. God is always happy when we are in the church that He has assigned us to. It pleases Him when we can honor him above family and friends to get where we belong. One of the first ways to honor God is to allow Him to assign us to a church. This is the will of God for your life and it has great rewards.

When God is pleased with us, we have favor in His sight. When we have favor in His sight, He causes us to have favor in every area of our lives. This favor is directly connected to us being set by God in the body of Christ. The first level of congregational favor begins when we join the church that God has for us. If God told you to join, nothing else matters.

The favor we receive for joining a church is called "Favor with God." There is not a greater favor for our lives than having favor with God. God controls all favor. He is the God of all grace and he uses it to bless those who join a church. Because joining a church brings us favor with God, let's take a look at what favor with God can do for us:

1. **Favor with God causes good to come into our lives.** *"For the Lord God is a sun and shield: the Lord will give grace and glory: no good thing will he withhold from them that walk uprightly"* (Psalms 84:11).

2. **Favor with God enriches our lives.** *"Grace be unto you, and peace, from God our Father, and from the Lord Jesus Christ. 4 I thank my God always on your behalf, for the grace of God which is given you by Jesus Christ; 5 That in every thing ye are enriched by him, in all utterance, and in all knowledge"* (1 Corinthians 1:3-5).

3. **Favor with God develops us into who we are called to be.** *"But by the grace of God I am what I*

am: and his grace which was bestowed upon me was not in vain; but I laboured more abundantly than they all: yet not I, but the grace of God which was with me." (1 Corinthians 15:10).

4. **Favor with God will bring us Favor with Man.** *"And Jesus increased in wisdom and stature, and in favour with God and man."* (Luke 2:52).

LIFE AND DEATH

The church you belong to is a matter of life and death. Deuteronomy 30:19 says, *"I call heaven and earth to record this day against you, that I have set before you life and death, blessing and cursing: therefore choose life, that both thou and thy seed may live."* God will only give you choices regarding your church membership. He will not make the decision for you. He does not interfere with free will. When you make the right decision, you will have favor. However, if you join the wrong church, you and your family will dry-up spiritually.

Immediately upon joining a church, God is pleased. Thus, we receive favor in the eyes of God and His grace begins to operate on our lives. It doesn't stop there; let's look at the next benefit that God has for us when we join a church.

2. JOINING CHURCH PLACES YOU IN POSITION TO BE ESTABLISHED

God wants His children to become established in life and in the Lord. He has provided a plan to ensure that this happens. It is available for every believer. When we join a church, we are placing ourselves in position to become established. In Acts 16:5 we read the following:

> And so were the churches established in the faith, and increased in number daily.

According to the Strong's Talking Greek & Hebrew Dictionary, the Greek word for Establish is "Stereoo". It means to *solidify, confirm*, receive strength, make strong. Likewise, the Hebrew word is "Qum". It means to be firm, fixed, stable, and secure.

When the church mentioned in the book of Acts became *"established"*, it's really referring to the church becoming solid, strong, firm, fixed, stable and secure. That's a lot of benefits just for joining a church. Look at it this way, any established church exists because its members are strong, firm stable and secure. When God makes you strong, you can make someone else strong. He has a vested interest in your success.

God used congregational favor to establish His people. In 1 Peter 5:10-11, Peter promises that God will use grace (favor) to establish the church members to whom he is speaking.

> But the God of all grace, who hath called us unto his eternal glory by Christ Jesus, after that ye have suffered a while, make you perfect, stablish, strengthen, settle *you*. 11 To him *be* glory and dominion for ever and ever. Amen.

God gets the glory when we are established because there is no better person to represent God than a successful Christian who did it God's way. A successful Christian has a successful testimony. A successful testimony creates a successful witnessing tool. A successful witnessing tool will convert people to Christ successfully. A successful convert, connected to a successful Christian, who joins a successful church, will grow into a successful Christian with a successful testimony and so on. It's a successful cycle.

People who are established do not find themselves moving from city to city when they feel like they can't make it anymore. They are not on drugs. They do not have to beg for money, food, clothing and shelter. They are not filing for divorce, quitting school and constantly losing jobs. They are not bogged down with debt. They are victorious over the devil and they don't run back to the same sin they have been delivered from. God gets the glory from their lives. It takes Congregational Favor to become established like this.

The church is a place that helps people get established. It does not always do this by paying their bills or providing everything that person needs to survive. If a man doesn't work, he shouldn't eat (2 Thessalonians 3:10). The church provides the spiritual food necessary for you to grow spiritually so you can become an established person who can help others become equally established.

Why Everyone Needs a Pastor

According to Eph 4:11-15, we need a pastor for the following reasons

1. So You Can Be Perfected and Furnished for Life
2. To Be Trained to do the Work of the Ministry
3. So You Can Be Edified or Made Strong
4. To Become Unified in Faith with Other Believers
5. So You Can Learn all of the knowledge of the Son of God
6. So You Can Be a Perfect or Complete Person Morally
7. To Measure up to stature (maturity) of Christ
8. So You Will not be a Child
9. So You Will not be Wishy-washy
10. So You Will Grow up in Christ

Joining a church is the first step to becoming established. When you become strong you can help someone else. We saw what the Book of Acts said, *"...and increased in number daily"*. People are added to established churches. People are added to churches where people are becoming solid, strong, firm, fixed, stable and secure.

I was not an established person when I moved my family to Jackson, Mississippi. I remember a time that I needed assistance and went to my church and they did not help me. Somehow God still worked my situation out and I made it. I did not get offended. Instead, I stayed at that same church several years until I relocated to Georgia. Because I remained faithful, I was never in a situation where I needed to depend on the church again. Even when hard times came, I was able to make it through by faith. Eventually, I became a resource available to help others.

When you join a church you are making yourself available for Congregational Favor to cause you to become established in life.

3. JOINING A CHURCH GIVES YOU POTENTIAL TO HAVE A SUCCESSFUL CAREER

When you join a church, you now have the potential of that church added to your career potential. If God is going to establish that church, He has to establish you and the other members of that church. He is a master of increasing the potential of His children. Moses was the leader of God's congregation as they were in bondage in

Egypt. Look at the potential Moses gained while he was involved with God's congregation.

And the Lord gave the people favour in the sight of the Egyptians. Moreover the man Moses *was* very great in the land of Egypt, in the sight of Pharaoh's servants, and in the sight of the people. In Exodus 11:3, God made Moses great in the eyes of Pharaoh's servants and the Egyptian people. The Egyptian people respected Moses more than they respected Pharaoh. If they didn't fear being killed, they probably would have made Moses the king. God blessed Moses because His congregation needed him to be successful so they could be successfully released from bondage. This is the same reason why God will bless you. He wants His children to have jobs, businesses, homes, good college educations and much more.

When he places His faithful people in positions of authority, they can help His children gain access to better opportunities, ultimately enhancing the church. God wants His people to have an overall better life. Better lives mean wealthier people, increased tithes and offerings and better churches. This increases the church's ability to establish God's Kingdom on the earth.

Someone might say, *"I am a nobody. I don't have any qualifications to be a CEO or a businessman or businesswoman."* Don't look at your qualifications in the natural. When you do what God wants you to do, your qualifications are spiritually based as much as they are natural. It's not only your résumé that wins you the job;

it's also your revelation that wins you the job. God can use one act of obedience to be the key to your success. Notice what He says in Psalms 113:7-8:

> He raiseth up the poor out of the dust, *and* lifteth the needy out of the dunghill; **8** That he may set *him* with princes, *even* with the princes of his people.

God can take the lowest of people and place them with the highest class of people in the world. You are one act of God away from the position you need to be in to bless God's church. Did you notice that God specializes in taking people who are not qualified and making them successful? When you join a church, your membership becomes your qualification for success. Whatever God wants to do for that church, He has to use the members to accomplish it. Notice this next scripture found in 1 Corinthians 1:26-31:

> For ye see your calling, brethren, how that not many wise men after the flesh, not many mighty, not many noble, *are called*: **27** But God hath chosen the foolish things of the world to confound the wise; and God hath chosen the weak things of the world to confound the things which are mighty; **28** And base things of the world, and things which are despised, hath God

chosen, *yea,* and things which are not, to bring to nought things that are: **29** That no flesh should glory in his presence. **30** But of him are ye in Christ Jesus, who of God is made unto us wisdom, and righteousness, and sanctification, and redemption: **31** That, according as it is written, He that glorieth, let him glory in the Lord.

Here is God again taking people who do not qualify for anything and raising them up. This time He tells us the reason in verse 29 *"That no flesh should glory in his presence"*. In other words, He wants to be glorified for raising up someone rather than someone coming into His church already raised up doing some great act, and stealing His glory. So the most qualified person to become a successful CEO or President of a company is the person who joins a church. Look at another scripture with me.

Their children also shall be as aforetime, and their congregation shall be established before me, and I will punish all that oppress them. **21** And their nobles shall be of themselves, and their governor shall proceed from the midst of them; and I will cause him to draw near, and he shall approach unto me: for who *is* this that engaged his heart to approach unto me?

saith the Lord. **22** And ye shall be my people, and I will be your God. Jeremiah 30:20-22

This time, God specifically notes that He is speaking about a congregation. He says He will establish it and punish those who oppress them. Reading further, He says their "nobles" shall be of themselves and "their" governor shall proceed from the midst of them. The word "nobles" means stately people, great people or people high in rank. God says these people are supposed to come out of the congregation. These people are developed spiritually. Their degree did not make them special. It can help but it takes God to do it.

Why Some People Never Join a Church
1. Past hurts.
2. Someone told them not to join
3. Former members gave them the "bad news" about the church
4. They don't want to make a commitment
5. They feel they have to be perfect to join
6. They don't know about the benefits of membership
7. They don't know God wants them to have a church

I have watched God raise me up from making $4.85 per hour while supporting a family of three, with nothing to my name, to Director of Elections for the State of Mississippi. He did this while I was a member of a good church. I did not qualify for the position I held in the natural, but God needed my tithes and offering to support His work in the earth. Therefore, He raised me up. He can do the same thing for you if you join a good church.

4. JOINING A CHURCH IS THE KEY TO ELIMINATING LACK IN YOUR LIFE

God takes care of His church members. When you connect with a church through membership, you become a part of the people who are cared for by God. He has always taken care of His congregation. In Deuteronomy 2:4-7, we see an example of God taking care of every member of His congregation.

> And command thou the people, saying, Ye *are* to pass through the coast of your brethren the children of Esau, which dwell in Seir; and they shall be afraid of you: take ye good heed unto yourselves therefore: **5** Meddle not with them; for I will not give you of their land, no, not so much as a foot breadth; because I have given mount Seir unto Esau *for* a possession. **6** Ye shall buy meat of them for money, that ye may eat; and ye shall also buy water of them for money, that ye may drink. **7** For the Lord thy God hath blessed thee in all the works of thy hand: he knoweth thy walking through this great

> wilderness: these forty years the Lord thy
> God *hath been* with thee; thou hast lacked
> nothing.

In verse 6, God reveals that He provided money for His church members to by food and drink. It was enough money for all of His children to eat. Also, He said that during their forty years in the wilderness, they had no lack. This is a great miracle of God's provision. Look at another scripture in Matthew 14:15-21:

> And when it was evening, his disciples
> came to him, saying, This is a desert place,
> and the time is now past; send the
> multitude away, that they may go into the
> villages, and buy themselves victuals.
> **16** But Jesus said unto them, They need
> not depart; give ye them to eat. **17** And
> they say unto him, We have here but five
> loaves, and two fishes. **18** Bring them
> hither to me. **19** And he commanded the
> multitude to sit down on the grass, and
> took the five loaves, and the two fishes,
> and looking up to heaven, he blessed, and
> brake, and gave the loaves to *his* disciples,
> and the disciples to the multitude. **20** And
> they did all eat, and were filled: and they
> took up of the fragments that remained
> twelve baskets full. **21** And they that had

eaten were about five thousand men, beside women and children.

This is a great testimony about God's provision. Jesus did not have to feed anyone. He had already performed miracles of healing in the previous verses. Instead of letting them provide for themselves, He decided to feed them. This was a very large congregation. In fact, it would be considered a mega-church today. In that day they only counted the men. Jesus fed approximately 15,000 people when you include women and children.

Because they were members of His congregation, He did not want them to have any lack. Besides, it would ruin the testimony for them to receive healing and then die of hunger on their journeys back to their homes. This is how God blesses you when you join a church. He will deliberately care for you make sure your needs are met. He always takes care of His congregation.

5. JOINING A CHURCH OPENS THE DOOR TO YOU HAVING NOTHING FEEBLE AND NOTHING WEEK IN YOUR LIFE

When God brought the children of Israel out of Egypt, He referred to them many times as His congregation. This is a type and shadow of the church individually and collectively. When God brought them out, He consistently demonstrated His ability to take care of them in many ways. He provided a cloud to keep them cool in the day and a fire to keep them warm at night. He protected them from the evil other nations planned for them. He healed them from snake bites. He also kept their clothes and shoes from wearing out for 40 years. This is congregational favor at its best.

Still, there's something else God did that I find to be very awesome; He made sure they were strong and healthy. In Psalms 105:37, there's a recount of how the children of Israel came out of Egypt. Let's take a look at it:

> He brought them forth also with silver and gold: and *there was* not one feeble *person* among their tribes.

When you join a church and apply the principles of the Word of God, you are going to grow stronger in many ways. You will look back over your life and find that you will get to a place where your weak areas become stronger and stronger.

The children of Israel were slaves to the Egyptians for 400 years. They were beaten, deprived of good food and given the lesser quality standards of living. Nevertheless, they still came out strong and victorious. Once again, God takes care of His people! I like to tell my congregation to declare, "Nothing Feeble, Nothing Weak!"

One day someone mentioned to me that they believe in "Nothing Missing, Nothing Broken". I believe that also. However, it's only one part of a whole revelation. If you have "Nothing Missing and Nothing Broken" it could still be "feeble and weak." Broken and weak are not the same. Broken means it will not work. Feeble means it will not work properly. So make this confession with me and mean it from your heart, "I have Nothing Missing, Nothing Broken, Nothing Feeble, and Nothing Weak!" Say that three times and expect to see God honor it in your life.

God did this for the children of Israel. They were a good example of how He likes to care for His church. Joining a church opens the door for us to have nothing feeble and nothing weak.

6. JOINING A CHURCH GIVES YOU POWER AND AUTHORITY

And Simon Peter answered and said, Thou art the Christ, the Son of the living God. **17** And Jesus answered and said unto him, Blessed art thou, Simon Barjona: for flesh and blood hath not revealed *it* unto thee, but my Father which is in heaven. **18** And I say also unto thee, That thou art Peter, and upon this rock I will build my church; and the gates of hell shall not prevail against it. Matthew 16:16-18.

CONGREGATIONAL FAVOR

One of the most important benefits of joining a church is the ability to stop the gates of hell from preventing you from moving forward in life. Jesus said to Peter that when He builds His church, the gates of hell shall not prevail against it [His church]. The power is in belonging to a local church. Your membership in a local church is a type and shadow of your belonging to Jesus Christ universally. Jesus said that His church would be built on the premise that the strongest opposing power to mankind (hell) would not be strong enough to stop His church.

The gates of hell personify the power that hell has to keep people in bondage and darkness through the works of Satan. Joining a church gives you power to stop the devil from working his dark power in your life, your family and anyone else who will receive you.

You don't have to struggle with sin, addictions, strongholds, depression, sickness, poverty and lack any longer. These are only a few of the powers of darkness that Satan tries to burden God's people with. They are lies and violate the very Word of God that Jesus said His church was built on.

If you belong to a church, you are stronger than the gates of hell and Satan combined. Jesus also told us that His church would have power in Heaven and on earth. He said in Matthew 16:16-18, *"And I will give unto thee the keys of the kingdom of heaven: and whatsoever thou shalt bind on earth shall be bound in heaven: and whatsoever thou shalt loose on earth shall be loosed in heaven."* This is power that's available to those who join a church.

Of course, the devil doesn't want you to belong to a church. He will always try to make you think you can have power without commitment. Unfortunately, there are people who try to exercise this power outside of church membership, which often proves to be disastrous. Look at Acts 19:13-20 and see the results of people who do not belong to a church attempting to operate in the power of God without authority.

> Then certain of the vagabond Jews, exorcists, took upon them to call over them which had evil spirits the name of the Lord Jesus, saying, We adjure you by Jesus whom Paul preacheth. 14 And there were seven sons of *one* Sceva, a Jew, *and* chief of the priests, which did so. 15 And the evil spirit answered and said, Jesus I know, and Paul I know; but who are ye? 16 And the man in whom the evil spirit was leaped on them, and overcame them, and prevailed against them, so that they fled out of that house naked and wounded. 17 And this was known to all the Jews and Greeks also dwelling at Ephesus; and fear fell on them all, and the name of the Lord Jesus was magnified. 18 And many that believed came, and confessed, and shewed their deeds. 19 Many of them also which used

curious arts brought their books together, and burned them before all *men*: and they counted the price of them, and found *it* fifty thousand *pieces* of silver. **20** So mightily grew the word of God and prevailed.

They were referred to as "vagabond Jews". This meant they were wanderers. They were visitors. They were not official members. When you join a church, you become an authorized member. As vagabonds, they lacked the necessary authority to prevail against the gates of hell. In essence, the gates of hell prevailed against them.

After their defeat, verse 17 – 20 reveals that the real church prevailed against the gates of hell and the people who were involved in the curious arts of witchcraft and the occult. These people were delivered and set free by the power of the church. This power is available to you when you join the church.

7. JOINING A CHURCH RELEASES THE "ZION BLESSING" ON YOU

The final benefit I want to introduce to you is the Zion Blessing. This is a package of blessings designed to empower God's church members. Zion comes from the word Mount Zion in the Bible. Mount Zion is made up of the mountains that surround Jerusalem. These mountains practically turned the Jerusalem metro area into a sanctuary large enough to hold all the people of Israel. Hence, the city of Jerusalem became the largest church structure in the world.

Mount Zion is not just a super structure. It actually contains the favor of God as found in Psalms 102:13, *"Thou shalt arise, and have mercy upon Zion: for the time to favour her, yea, the set time, is come."* The Psalms go further to show how important Zion is to God in Psalms 132:13-16 where it says, *"For the Lord hath chosen Zion; he hath desired it for his habitation. 14 This is my rest for ever: here will I dwell; for I have desired it. 15 I will abundantly bless her provision: I will satisfy her poor with bread. 16 I will also clothe her priests with salvation: and her saints shall shout aloud for joy."*

God promised to place the Blessing of Zion on you when you become a member of a church. Look at Psalms 134:1-3:

> Behold, bless ye the Lord, all ye servants of the Lord, which by night stand in the house of the Lord. 2 Lift up your hands in the sanctuary, and bless the Lord. 3 The Lord that made heaven and earth bless thee out of Zion.

Are you ready to receive the Zion Blessing? When you join a church, you are in position to receive it. Here's a breakdown of the Zion Blessing that's available for you.

CONGREGATIONAL FAVOR

1.   Help in Trouble.   Psalms 20:1-2, *"The Lord hear thee in the day of trouble; the name of the God of Jacob defend thee; 2 Send thee help from the sanctuary, and strengthen thee out of Zion."*   The Zion Blessing contains help in your time of trouble.   When we join a church, there will be help and strength for us so we can make it through the storms of life and be victorious.

2.   Acceptance of Your Offerings.   Psalms 51:18-19, *"Do good in thy good pleasure unto Zion: build thou the walls of Jerusalem. 19 Then shalt thou be pleased with the sacrifices of righteousness, with burnt offering and whole burnt offering: then shall they offer bullocks upon thine altar."*   The Zion Blessing contains acceptance of your offering.   When you bring your offering into the church, God will respect it because you are a member of a church.

3.   Peace and Vitality.   Psalms 147:12-15, *"Praise the Lord, O Jerusalem; praise thy God, O Zion. 13 For he hath strengthened the bars of thy gates; he hath blessed thy children within thee. 14 He maketh peace in thy borders, and filleth thee with the finest of the wheat. 15 He sendeth forth his commandment upon earth: his word runneth very swiftly."*   There is peace and vitality in the Zion Blessing.   God's Word shows how everything works well in Zion.   He does the same for His church today.   When you join a church, you partake in a fertile environment with those who want their lives to have peace and liveliness.

4. Restoration. Jeremiah 30:17, *"For I will restore health unto thee, and I will heal thee of thy wounds, saith the Lord; because they called thee an Outcast, saying, This is Zion, whom no man seeketh after."* The Zion blessing causes restoration to manifest. God can restore health, wealth, prosperity, jobs, marriages, and so much more when you join a church.

5. The Good Life. Psalms 128:1-6, *"Blessed is every one that feareth the Lord; that walketh in his ways. 2 For thou shalt eat the labour of thine hands: happy shalt thou be, and it shall be well with thee. 3 Thy wife shall be as a fruitful vine by the sides of thine house: thy children like olive plants round about thy table. 4 Behold, that thus shall the man be blessed that feareth the Lord. 5 The Lord shall bless thee out of Zion: and thou shalt see the good of Jerusalem all the days of thy life. 6 Yea, thou shalt see thy children's children, and peace upon Israel."* The Zion Blessing contains the good life. When you join a church, this blessing makes your life good for you, your children and your grandchildren. It makes your wife fruitful and fertile. It makes your employment or business fruitful. It makes you happy emotionally and it makes everything well with you and your family.

6. Protection. Psalms 125:1-3, *"They that trust in the Lord shall be as mount Zion, which cannot be removed, but abideth for ever.* **2** *As the mountains are round about Jerusalem, so the Lord is round about his people from henceforth even for ever.* **3** *For the rod of the wicked shall not rest upon the lot of the righteous; lest the righteous put forth their hands unto iniquity."* The Zion Blessing contains protection. God protects the things He loves. When you join a church, you partake in the protection of God's presence on His church and its members.

Joining a church has so many benefits. When you make a decision to join, you will experience Congregational Favor on your life in every area. Make a quality decision to find a church for you and your family and join it. You will open the door to some great benefits and the favor of God will explode over your life.

Chapter 2

The Benefits of Church Attendance

. . . .

Once you join a church you are ready to walk in "congregational favor". There's another step you need to take to activate the favor of God that is on your life – You need to attend church regularly. By regularly, I mean every Sunday, mid-week service, conferences and all the special events that your church offers. God is interested in us being present. He has sweetened the deal for us to make it attractive for us be present. I call this the "Benefits of Attendance". It is simply the favor of God that comes upon us just for faithfully showing up and being present.

In this chapter, I want to introduce you to the benefits you receive from faithfully attending your church. You can look forward to the following benefits when you start attending church regularly:

CONGREGATIONAL FAVOR

1. CHURCH ATTENDANCE CAUSES THE WORD OF GOD TO PENETRATE YOUR ENTIRE LIFE

> Now it came to pass, as they went, that he entered into a certain village: and a certain woman named Martha received him into her house. 39 And she had a sister called Mary, which also sat at Jesus' feet, and heard his word. 40 But Martha was cumbered about much serving, and came to him, and said, Lord, dost thou not care that my sister hath left me to serve alone? bid her therefore that she help me. 41 And Jesus answered and said unto her, Martha, Martha, thou art careful and troubled about many things: 42 But one thing is needful: and Mary hath chosen that good part, which shall not be taken away from her. Luke 10:38-42

In church is where the Word penetrates your life. Mary was sitting a Jesus' feet. Technically, she was in church. We shouldn't go to the church merely for the fellowship, music and all the other amenities. These things are important. However, we should go mainly for the Word of God. The Word is what God deems most important. Psalms 138:2 says, *"I will worship toward thy holy temple, and praise thy name for thy lovingkindness and for thy truth: for thou hast magnified thy word above all thy name."* It's not important merely because God wants to say something. It's important because His Word is spiritually tangible. The Word of God can enter into your body, soul and spirit. In fact, it doesn't have any effect on your life until it enters you. In Psalms 119:130 it says, *"The **entrance** of thy words giveth light; it giveth understanding unto the simple."* You can hear the Word anywhere, but when you hear it in church, it penetrates your life. Jesus said what Mary was receiving would not be taken away. That means it penetrated her life. Here is the process:

1. When you hear the Word in church, it enters your life.
2. When it enters your body it unfolds like a seed and begins to grow faith in your heart.
3. When it unfolds as faith, it begins to grow into the very thing you need or believed for.

Hearing the Word is not enough. It must penetrate to be effective. I had my carpet cleaned and decided to have Scotch Guard put on the carpet to help keep it clean. One day my son Jeremy came in the house with mud on his shoes. I was upset at first but I remembered that I had the cleaning company put Scotch Guard on the carpet. I then told him to let it dry and I would vacuum it. This worked perfectly because the mud did not penetrate.

The devil's plan is to keep you at a place where the Word of God will not penetrate. He tries to Scotch Guard your life. He does this by encouraging you to miss church. When you come into the house of God, the praise and worship and corporate prayer, are just some of the things that will cause the preached Word of God to penetrate.

Don't be a wayside hearer. A wayside hearer hears the Word, listens to the Word, even talks about the Word. However, the Word never penetrates because they are only listening from the sidelines. They are not listening to it in the church, from the preacher.

You can receive the Word in every format imaginable – mp3, DVD, CD, magazine, text, email, internet, television, radio, IPod, IPad, e Reader, electronic bibles, etc and you will learn some valuable lessons. However, the Word will never penetrate you until you go to an actual church service and hear it from the man or woman of God. Romans 10:17 says, *"So then faith cometh by hearing, and hearing by the word of God."* It also says in Romans 10:14 *"... and how shall they hear without a preacher?"*

2. ATTENDING CHURCH HELPS YOU GET FOCUSED AND AVOID DISTRACTIONS

Focus is an important key to successful living. Ask any person who is serious about success and they will tell you to get focused and stay focused. For successful

Christian living, you must remain focused regardless of the circumstances, distractions and opportunities that you face in life. David, while writing Psalm 122, gave us a secret to staying focused as a Christian.

> Psalms 122:1 I was glad when they said unto me, Let us go into the house of the LORD.

> Psalms 122:9 Because of the house of the LORD our God I will seek thy good.

For the most part, David understood that the cause of him staying focused on God's goodness was "The house of the Lord". People become distracted when they are not in the house of God. Being in the house of God helps us to gain and keep our focus on the will of God for our lives. Attendance helps get focus in three ways:

a. ***By allowing us to hear the Word.*** The Word of God becomes a focal point in our lives. Therefore, when we are about to miss the mark, the Word that we heard preached while we were in church, helps us to make the right decisions for our lives.

b. ***By allowing other Christians to provoke us to good works.*** We need other people whether we believe it or not. Their provoking us is like peer pressure. It makes us want to do our best. Thus, we always want to make a good impression for our spiritual family. David said, *"I was glad when they said unto me...."* You need someone else to help keep you on track.

c. By being accountable to someone you respect. Everyone should have someone they respect and want to please. Your pastor is that person. Since he represents God's authority in the earth, you should have a pastor to be accountable to. It's important for him to know that the Word of God is working in your life.

I have seen people come to church with nothing to their name but problems and troubles. After a period of time, I have watched them start attending services, begin tithing and become active participants in church to the point where their lives have changed for the better. Sadly however, I have seen others become successful financially only to lose it when they stopped attending church. I have seen some go back to a life of drug addictions, family problems and other things they were delivered from all because they stopped attending church and they lost focus. Stay in church and keep your focus.

3. CHURCH ATTENDANCE MAKES YOU STRONG

When a person is not in the church for a period of time, they become spiritually weak. Psalms 84:2 says, *"My soul longeth, yea, even fainteth for the courts of the LORD: my heart and my flesh crieth out for the living God."* Many times, spiritual fatigue is the cause for failure in the body of Christ. Too many Christians do not have the might to handle the temptations, tests and trials they face in life. When they do finally come to church, it is because they are at a point where they are spiritually faint. A spiritually faint person is like a person who is starving. He will make an effort to get some food. Nevertheless, as soon as they get a meal they wander away from the church until they find themselves faint again. It's a vicious cycle that's causing Christians to loose the battles of life.

Strength is very important in our natural and spiritual lives. I was going through a physical battle in my life once and I thought I was eating very healthy – I was eating only meat and vegetables. My wife came to me and said that I was probably weak because of the foods I was eating. She told me I probably needed to eat some good old fashioned, down home cooking. I thought I would test her theory out so I ate a good old-fashioned meal and found that she was right. The food I ate gave me the strength I needed to get moving.

CONGREGATIONAL FAVOR

You cannot push through the storm or move the mountain if you are weak. Not having enough spiritual food will make your faith weak. When you receive spiritual food into your life, it will become easier for you to overcome your problems. When we fill our schedules up with football practice, soccer and all the extracurricular activities that our children's schools provide, we gain no strength or added value. It's like eating a meal with no starchy carbohydrates and no protein. Yes you can lose weight doing it that way, but you will eventually become very weak. The body needs some carbohydrates and some protein to give you energy. Likewise, your spirit needs church attendance to make and keep you strong. God will favor you with strength when you come into His house.

How much church should a person attend? Just like eating, you need two or three meals per day and few healthy snacks in between to stay strong. I believe to stay spiritually strong you need two to three meals per week and a snack daily. The meals are the spiritual feedings you get when you attend the church. The snacks are your daily devotionals or teachings that you read, listen to or watch.

If we are not careful, we will allow our families to become weak through their daily activities and never take the time to get them filled spiritually. For instance, sports have become a major part of our society. Football practices almost every day for many schools. I have had to tell my children's coaches that my children would not be able to participate on Wednesday evenings due to church attendance. It was not much they could say, but I could tell this did not go over very well. Nevertheless, I realized that whatever my children devote most of their time to is going to be their god. If I'm giving them Monday, Tuesday, Thursday and Friday; two hours per day all summer and during the first half of the school year, it's fair to assume, they will become proficient at football. They learn the "Playbook" but not the "Good-book." Therefore, I decided that my children needed to be in church on Wednesday.

4. CHURCH ATTENDANCE EMPOWERS YOU FOR SUCCESS AND VICTORY

Blessed *are* they that dwell in thy house:
they will be still praising thee. Selah.
Blessed *is* the man whose strength *is* in
thee; in whose heart *are* the ways *of them.*
Psalms 84:4-5

The Word blessed means "Empowered for Success and Victory." The person who dwells in the house of God is "empowered and enabled" to have success in their life. They can overcome trials, troubles or tribulations. They are empowered to succeed and soar in life. This is the empowerment that only comes from being present physically in the church. Also, they will be able to praise the Lord and walk in joy when they are in the midst of trials, troubles or tribulations.

This "blessing" is specifically limited to "they that dwell in thy house" as the Psalm says. Those who do not attend church, they will not have this blessing. They will not be enabled. In essence, they will be cursed. To be cursed means to have no empowerment and no enablement. Instead of being enabled, to be cursed means to have their spiritual power disabled. To be cursed means to have no power during the trial, trouble or tribulation. There are too many cursed, powerless, disabled Christians.

Finding a Mentor in Your Church

As you start attending church, you might decide you need a mentor to help you grow. Here is what you look for:

1. Mentors Train People for the Lord's Work - Matt 10:1
2. Mentors Protect from False Doctrines - Matt 16:5-12
3. Mentors Teach Others how to Pray - Matt 26:36-46
4. Mentors Train others for Leadership - Matt 14:15-19
5. Mentors Teach Others to Win Souls - Matt 9:37-38
6. Mentors Lead by Example - 1 Tim 4:12
7. A Mentors is Impartial - 1 Tim 5:21
8. Mentors Teach Others to Bear Fruit - John 15:7-8
9. Mentors Help Others Learn the Culture - 1 Tim 3:15
10. Mentors Show Others How to Win - Matt 17:19-21
11. Mentors Teach Others to be Involved - Acts 6:1-4
12. A Mentor is Available - Matt 5:1-2
13. Mentors Dispel Division - Matt 20:20-27
14. A Mentor Joins People to the Church - Acts 9:26-28
15. Mentors Inherit the Promises of God - Heb 6:12

Blessings don't last forever. They have an expiration date. They always end when you stop the process. In Malachi chapter 3, God said that when you tithe, He will pour you out a blessing. "A Blessing" means one blessing. That one blessing will last until you have the opportunity to tithe again. When you get the opportunity to tithe again and you decide not to tithe, the blessing expires. The blessing that comes with church attendance will start when you start attending church and will last until you decide not to attend church anymore. When you decide not to attend church any longer, the blessing will stop. Start attending church and don't ever stop so you can walk in the blessing.

5. CHURCH ATTENDANCE IS 1,000 TIMES MORE EFFECTIVE THAN ANYTHING ELSE YOU CAN DO TO BETTER YOUR LIFE

There are so many things that we can do to better ourselves in this life. We can further our education, workout and exercise, read books, learn a trade or hobby, or even eat better to name a few. However, no matter what we do to better ourselves, the Word of God teaches us that nothing will do more for us than just one day in the house of God. In Psalms 84:10, *"For a day in thy courts is better than a thousand. I had rather be a doorkeeper in the house of my God, than to dwell in the tents of wickedness."* Notice that he does not tell us a thousand of what. He cannot be referring to a thousand days because that would mean all we would ever need was one day for our entire life. He left it up to us to do our own comparison. It doesn't matter what the "what" is, one day in the church is more effective for your life than anything you can do to better yourself.

If you post your résumé on one thousand employment websites, it still will not compare to the potential of the regular church attendee who post their résumé on one employment website. There was a member of our church who did not have a job. She was unemployed for five months. She had sent several résumés to many companies over that time period but still was unemployed. During one of our weekly church services, she was in the children's ministry as I walked pass. I said to her in passing, "your job just opened up". She replied "Thank you Pastor" with a very grateful tone. Three weeks later she was employed. What if she had not been there to receive that prophecy? Her breakthrough depended on her church attendance not her résumé. Whenever you think about not showing up for church, ask yourself this question: "If I miss church, what am I going to miss?"

Church attendance is 1,000 times better than my résumé. It is 1000 times better than my loan application. It is 1000 times better than my paycheck. It is 1000 times better than my car loan application. It is 1000 times better than my 401K. Do you get the picture? Church attendance is 1,000 times better than anything you can do to get progress in your life.

6. CHURCH ATTENDANCE MAKES YOU LIKE JESUS CHRIST

> Acts 11:25-26 Then departed Barnabas to Tarsus, for to seek Saul: **26** And when he had found him, he brought him unto Antioch. And it came to pass, that a whole year they assembled themselves with the church, and taught much people. And the disciples were called Christians first in Antioch.

Church attendance transforms you into a Christian by developing your mind and your character. When your mind and character is developed, your actions will follow. Just because a person is born-again doesn't mean they have Christian character and actions. It takes time around other Christians to develop Christian character. The word Christian means "Christ-like". The more time we spend in church, the more we look like Christ. It took an entire year with Barnabas and Saul before the Antioch church members were identified by the community as Christians. They were already born-again but no one recognized that they were Christ-like. You will begin to change when you become acquainted with role models in the church.

Notice they were taught by Barnabas and Saul (Paul). God uses the Pastor to change His sheep into all He called them to be. Pastors are important to your success. It's equally important that you hear the Word from your Pastor every week. God calls us His sheep and refers to pastors as shepherds. Shepherds take care of the sheep. They sheer the sheep, feed the sheep, protect the sheep and nurture the sheep. Just like a shepherd over the sheep, God assigns pastors to do these things for you so you can become like Jesus Christ.

When you sit under your pastor's teaching, you are being sheered from all your tangled wooly ways. You are being fed the Word of God, protected from the devil and nurtured by God. When you fail to attend church, you are like the sheep who wanders from the sheepfold.

When we first come to Christ, we don't act much like Jesus. Unfortunately, for many Christians they don't conform to His likeness because they don't do anything to change. If you want to become like Christ, you have to shed the old nature so you can take on the new nature Christ has given you. This conversion is not done simply by changing clothes or fixing your hair a certain way; it's done, in part, by attending church. When you take time to go into the house of God, you are taught by the pastor how to take on the nature of Christ.

7. CHURCH ATTENDANCE CAUSE GOODNESS AND MERCY TO FOLLOW YOU DAILY

Goodness and mercy are in the house of the Lord. Psalms 23:5-6 says, *"Surely goodness and mercy shall follow me all the days of my life: and I will dwell in the house of the LORD for ever."* When I attend church, goodness and mercy is going to follow me. Goodness always follows a person who attends church. When I make a mistake, mercy is there to catch me. This special help follows me all the days of my life as I dwell in the house of the Lord. This special privilege is relative. As long as I am dwelling in His house, goodness and mercy is there for me. When I stop attending church, I begin to miss out on goodness and mercy.

What does attending church have to do with the goodness and mercy of God? God has a multitude of mercies that are physically located in His church buildings. In Malachi 3:10 God says, *"Bring ye all the tithes into the storehouse..."* The church is the storehouse. It's not a storehouse for natural things; but a storehouse for spiritual things. It stores the mercies of God, and plenty of it. Psalms 5:7 says, *"But as for me, I will come into thy house in the multitude of thy mercy: and in thy fear will I worship toward thy holy temple."* Notice that the mercies are literally located in the building.

CONGREGATIONAL FAVOR

How did the goodness and mercy of God get there? Goodness and mercy is there because God put it there. When a church is built, it takes the hard earned money of the members to build it. Also, it takes the dedication of faithful church volunteers and workers. It takes the committed direction and prayers of the pastors and leaders. So much time and effort goes into the building of the church that God honors this commitment by providing His stamp of approval on the building through the outpouring of His goodness and mercy.

If you have messed up in life, there is goodness and mercy in your church. If you need forgiveness, there is goodness and mercy in your church. Attending church makes the goodness and mercy of God available. But remember, it's not only for when things go wrong. Goodness and mercy is also available for when you want to intentionally make things to go right. Psalms 65:4 says, "... we shall be satisfied with the goodness of thy house, even of thy holy temple." There is goodness physically located in the house of God. What's even better is He wants to "satisfy" us with this goodness. We get God's goodness and mercy when we show up to church. We are surrounded by God's goodness and mercy when we attend church.

8. CHURCH ATTENDANCE BRINGS YOU PROTECTION

> One thing have I desired of the LORD, that will I seek after; that I may dwell in the house of the LORD all the days of my life, to behold the beauty of the LORD, and to inquire in his temple. 5 For in the time of trouble he shall hide me in his pavilion: in the secret of his tabernacle shall he hide me; he shall set me up upon a rock. 6 And now shall mine head be lifted up above mine enemies round about me: therefore will I offer in his tabernacle sacrifices of joy; I will sing, yea, I will sing praises unto the LORD. Psalms 27:4-6

Once again we see the favor of God connected to being in the house of the Lord. This time, we see the protection of the Lord associated with being in His house. When we make it a habit of going into the house of the Lord under the direction of a local pastor, God intentionally gets involved in making us safe. David fought many deadly battles. He was a warrior and a man of blood. If anyone understood the need for protection, David did. He connects his protection to attending church.

We might never fully understand the connection of church attendance and God's protection, but we should begin to allow it to operate in our lives. This scripture is a model or blueprint regarding our protection. It is a parallel truth like baptism. In short, when we are baptized, we are saying to the world that we died and were buried like Christ. When we come out of the water, we are saying to the world we are raised like Christ when He was raised from the dead. God established this system for us to simulate this process and He honors it in our lives.

Here's another parallel, when we attend church services, we are showing the Lord that we are hiding in His pavilion for safety. It's an expression of our faith. Just as we present ourselves to the Lord as hiding in His pavilion, He can match our faith with His protection. David said He "shall" hide me. His faith was very strong in believing that if He stayed in the temple, God would see his faith and reward him with protection.

Many times people don't attend their mid-week evening services because they fear being out at night. Don't be afraid! Expect the favor of God. He wants you to attend your church services. He will provide the protection.

9. CHURCH ATTENDANCE MAKES YOU PROSPEROUS NATURALLY AND SPIRITUALLY

Psalms 52:8-9 But I *am* like a green olive tree in the house of God: I trust in the mercy of God for ever and ever. 9 I will praise thee for ever, because thou hast done *it*: and I will wait on thy name; for *it is* good before thy saints.

Easton's Illustrated Dictionary refers to the olive tree as an "emblem of prosperity, beauty and religious privilege." When David wrote this psalm, he was identifying the temple of God as the source of his prosperity and spiritual maturity. By nature, the olive tree grows wild out in the natural elements. The olive tree that was planted in the house of God was catered to and cared for. It was kept out of the cold and extreme heat and it was nurtured by the gardeners of the house of God.

The olive tree is known for two things: The fruit it bears (olives) and the product the fruit yields - olive oil. The olives represent prosperity and the oil represents spiritual maturity.

When you are planted in your local church, you have the potential to produce fruit in life. That's prosperity in every area of your life. Your attendance in church, if the Word of God is being taught there, will activate the prosperity of God in your life. It will cause your family to prosper spiritually, physically and mentally. You will be in position to receive a better all-around life. That's what prosperity is; a better all-around life. It's being debt-free, having the level of wealth you need to enjoy, being able to further the Gospel, having a good marriage, responsible teenagers, obedient children, a good education, a pleasant neighborhood and victory over trials.

Church attendance will help you become spiritually mature. When you attend, you avail yourself to learning and developing in the spiritual gifts. You also learn how to yield your natural gifts and talents to the anointing. The church is the greatest training ground for God's people. He does not use school, college and employee training programs to make His people skilled in the anointing; He uses His church. You can have many gifts that can be properly trained in the world's system. They will work well in that system; but without the anointing on those gifts, they will not change lives for the kingdom of God.

If you want to become prosperous and mature in every area of your life, attending church is the ultimate key to your success.

10. CHURCH ATTENDANCE ALLOWS YOU TO EXPERIENCE THE POWER OF PRAISE

Praise is an expression of our admiration and adoration for our God and the things He has done in the earth. We can praise the Lord at home or anytime we feel like expressing our love and appreciation to Him. The psalmist gives us a secret to unleashing maximum power in Psalms 89:15-18:

Blessed is the people that know the joyful sound: they shall walk, O Lord, in the light of thy countenance. 16 In thy name shall they rejoice all the day: and in thy righteousness shall they be exalted. 17 For thou art the glory of their strength: and in thy favour our horn shall be exalted. 18 For the Lord is our defence; and the Holy One of Israel is our king.

According to this verse, when righteous people praise the Lord they experience 4 things:

1. The Light of God's Countenance. This is Favor in the sight of God. This means He is pleased with our praises and worship.
2. Exaltation. We can expect promotion in our lives.
3. Glory and Strength. We can expect God to be the source of our physical well-being.
4. Horn Exalted. We can expect visibility and notoriety to happen in our lives as we praise Him.

As you can see, there is great power in Praise. In Psalms 107:31-32, we receive a lesson on how to increase the magnitude of this same power exponentially.

"Oh that *men* would praise the Lord *for* his goodness, and *for* his wonderful works to the children of men! 32 Let them exalt him also in the congregation of the people, and praise him in the assembly of the elders."

The key is attending the praise and worship session at church. This allows the entire congregation to praise God with the power of agreement. The power of agreement will cause the impact of praise and worship to be multiplied exponentially.

Why People Leave a Church Prematurely

Here are several reasons why people leave their church prematurely.

1. They Don't Feel Connected
2. They Get Offended by Someone
3. They Get Offended by the Pastor
4. They Get Offered an Opportunity at Another Church
5. They Get Tempted by the World
6. They Fail to Balance their Work Schedule with God
7. They Forget that God Placed them in the Local Church
8. They Receive an Untimely Call to Ministry
9. They Refuse to Submit to Leadership
10. Their Family or Friends Leave
11. They Listen to Negative Influences

Don't allow these wrong motives to influence your decisions.

Praise and worship is not a private affair. It was intended to be a public expression of your gratitude towards God. It brings great power when we do it as a group. It's an awesome way to join your faith with the faith of others and experience the power of God in a shared environment. Your benefits become their benefits and their benefits become yours. In the Book of

Leviticus, God's Word shares the power of His people working together.

> And five of you shall chase an hundred, and an hundred of you shall put ten thousand to flight: and your enemies shall fall before you by the sword. 9 For I will have respect unto you, and make you fruitful, and multiply you, and establish my covenant with you. Leviticus 26:8-9.

God demonstrates this power again in 2 Chronicles 20:20-30 by having his people praise God instead of fighting during a war. They won the battle by using praise and worship congregationally. There is favor when we praise God in the congregation. If you want to see greater victories in your life, make sure you attend the praise and worship sessions at your church.

11. CHURCH ATTENDANCE ALLOWS YOUR PASTOR TO BLESS YOU

To bless means to speak something good about someone. In today's times, with so much evil happening in the world, it's important that we receive blessings from our pastors every week. In Psalms 118:26, we see an example of the blessing that comes from being in the house of God.

> Blessed *be* he that cometh in the name of .
> the Lord: we have blessed you out of the
> house of the Lord.

While there is nothing wrong with being blessed by the people you know, every person should have the experience of the pastor's blessing. When you are blessed by your pastor, He stands in the authority of God. It carries great weight. He is authorized to bless God's people.

Let's look at the blessing being released by people of two different offices in society; first David the king and then the priest and Levites (God's ministers). Look at the blessing released by David on the congregation in 1 Chronicles 16:2.

> And when David had made an end of
> offering the burnt offerings and the peace
> offerings, he blessed the people in the
> name of the Lord.

Next, we will see the blessing released by the God's priests and the Levites in 2 Chronicles 30:27.

> Then the priests the Levites arose and
> blessed the people: and their voice was
> heard, and their prayer came *up* to his holy
> dwelling place, *even* unto heaven.

Both blessings carried great weight. But when the priest and Levites blessed the people, the Bible says that their prayer went up into heaven. David blessed the people in the Name of the Lord but he was not a priest or a Levite. The blessing of the priests and Levites is the same as the blessing of the Pastor. God will honor the blessing of His pastors when they speak over your life. You can have many people speak good things over your life, but when the pastor speaks good things over you, it's honored by God.

When you attend your church services, the pastor may release blessings at different times during his lesson. There is power in the blessing for those who are in attendance. Even if you are going to be late, which I do not recommend, go anyway so you can at least receive the blessing during the benediction. You need the goodness of God spoken over your life to combat all the evil this world offers.

12. ATTENDANCE BRINGS YOU DIRECTLY INTO THE PRESENCE AND POWER OF THE LORD

One of the greatest attacks on the people today is emotional instability. Stress, worry, anxiety, fear, depression and so many more attacks are plaguing the people of the world and even the children of God. It's easy to understand why the children of the world would have these emotional problems but the church should be victorious emotionally. What is happening emotionally? Many Christians have forgotten that joy comes from the Lord and that it belongs to us regardless of the circumstances.

The key to emotional stability is having the joy of the Lord. We have the joy of the Lord when we get in His presence. In Psalms 16:11 it says, "…in thy presence *is* fulness of joy; at thy right hand *there are* pleasures for evermore." We must get into the presence of God to defeat all of our emotional attacks.

When we attend church services, we get directly into the presence of God. According to Matthew 18:20, *"For where two or three are gathered together in my name, there am I in the midst of them."* When we go to church there are at least two or three present. In fact, you cannot have church unless there are two or three present. So you cannot have church at home by yourself. Jesus clearly says when we have two or three gathered together in His Name, He is in the midst of us.

Don't discount the importance of experiencing God's presence in church. Notice Exodus 25:8, *"And let them make me a sanctuary; that I may dwell among them."* God wanted the sanctuary built so He could dwell in it. We know that we are the temple of the Holy Spirit, but obviously there is the presence of the Lord at church as well. He's also there because we are there. When we come to church, each individual believer brings the Holy Spirit with them to church.

The Benefits of Church Attendance

If you want to experience the presence of the Lord, you need to show up at your church service regularly. There's more than just experiencing the presence of the Lord, there is also the power of God awaiting you at the church. Look at 2 Chronicles 5:13-14:

> It came even to pass, as the trumpeters and singers *were* as one, to make one sound to be heard in praising and thanking the Lord; and when they lifted up *their* voice with the trumpets and cymbals and instruments of musick, and praised the Lord, *saying*, For *he is* good; for his mercy *endureth* for ever: that *then* the house was filled with a cloud, *even* the house of the Lord; 14 So that the priests could not stand to minister by reason of the cloud: for the glory of the Lord had filled the house of God.

Notice the people came to the house of God and the presence of the Lord was there. See also how the glory of God manifested in the house of the Lord. The Glory of the Lord was the power of God. When we go to church, the power of God will be present to move in our lives. This is where healing, miracles, signs and wonders take place. I have seen great healings take place in the lives of the people who attend church. If you want to experience the presence and see the power of God, you must attend your church services regularly.

13. CHURCH ATTENDANCE BRINGS YOU THE HONOR OF GOD

The Lord should be glorified in your life. If you really want to give Him glory, you must attend church regularly. Private glory is not enough to say "thank you" to the Lord for all He has done for you. There are some things that God wants done publicly. Baptism is a public display of your salvation. God designed baptism so that He would be glorified before men when you are born-again. Jesus said let men see your good works so they can glorify your God (Matthew 5:16).

There is a time and a place for publicly glorifying God. It's at your regularly scheduled church services. This is the perfect place and time to publicly glorify God. Look at Psalms 96:6-8:

> Honour and majesty *are* before him: strength and beauty *are* in his sanctuary. **7** Give unto the Lord, O ye kindreds of the people, give unto the Lord glory and strength. **8** Give unto the Lord the glory *due unto* his name: bring an offering, and come into his courts.

The Benefits of Church Attendance

The word "Glory" means "honor" in the Old Testament. When we attend church, we honor God publicly. When we give in church, we honor God publicly. When we serve in church, we honor God publicly. Here is how your attendance honors God publicly: Your attendance states to all of heaven and earth that nothing is more important to you than Jesus, your relationship to God, and the advancement of the kingdom of God in the earth. God takes an account of this honor and receives it.

We are not only Honoring God when we go to church but we are receiving honor when we attend church. There is honor in the actual church building stored up for us. We see this when we read Psalms 26:8, "Lord, I have loved the habitation of thy house, and the place where thine honour dwelleth." Notice the honor of God is in God's house. The church building is God's house according to Paul in 1 Timothy 3:15 which says, *"But if I tarry long, that thou mayest know how thou oughtest to behave thyself in the house of God, which is the church of the living God, the pillar and ground of the truth."*

When we honor God by attending church, He will honor us. 1 Samuel 2:30 says, *"...for them that honour me I will honour, and they that despise me shall be lightly esteemed."* When we honor God, He returns the favor in our lives. When we despise coming to church we despise Him. In the New Testament, the word "honor" means "value". When you "value" the Lord, He will "value" you. If you would like to increase your value, increase your honor towards the Lord by attending church regularly.

Top 10 Excuses People use to Miss Church

1. **It's Raining.** *If you come out in God's storm, He will come out in yours.*
2. **I'm Not Feeling Well.** *Run to the church for healing.*
3. **The Pastor is not there this week.** *You still need the Word.*
4. **I don't have transportation.** *People find a ride to work and everywhere else they want to go.*
5. **Church is Boring and Irrelevant.** *Find a church that is not boring.*
6. **I don't need that much church.** *Jesus went every week.*
7. **I don't have anything to wear.** *Find a church where you can come as you are.*
8. **I don't have any money to give.** *As you attend, you will increase financially so you can give.*
9. **I'm too tired.** *You will be inspired and energized as you attend.*
10. **I'm too busy.** *You will only be as busy as you allow yourself to be.*

14. CHURCH ATTENDANCE CHANGES THE WAY YOU THINK

Thinking controls everything that we do. Our thinking is always shaped by influences. Television, radio, music, friends, books, education, technology, and the environment all have a role to play in how we think. God wants to influence your thoughts. His influence in your life will determine how you will perform as His child. Look at Psalms 48:9:

> We have thought of thy lovingkindness, O
> God, in the midst of thy temple.

When we go to the local church, we open ourselves up to learn the Word of God in a fashion that will allow us to develop proper thinking patterns. We will begin to think like a winner. If we are hearing the right words, we will think thoughts that will influence our decision-making and allow us to prosper in every area of life. It's not only the Word that helps change our thinking; there are many other influences in the local church that contribute to this. Here are a few things that shape and impact the way you think:

1.   **People.** The first influence is the people at large. When you see others who are excited about Jesus Christ, you begin to measure your excitement level against theirs. This can result in a change in the way you think. Witnessing the blessings and hearing the testimonies of others, allows you to experience the goodness of God first hand.

2.   **Excellence.** You set standards of excellence in your life oftentimes by how your church portrays excellence. Once you see excellence, you will begin to

emulate it. Experiencing excellence is another way your thoughts are changed for the better.

3.   **Music.** Music is a powerful force in changing the mindset of people. One good praise song can embed a scripture in your mind that helps you overcome many obstacles for years to come.

4.   **Leaders.** When you see those who are skillful and successful in the things of God, it will inspire you to aim for opportunities to do the same.

5.   **Small Groups.** Bible Studies, Small Group Classes, even Sunday School has a great impact on the way you think. Grouping with people with like circumstances, helps you to enjoy fellowship, fun and growth together.

6.   **Bookstore.** This is a powerful mind-changing arena. It contains valuable ministry resources and other helpful aids to assist you in becoming a productive Christian.

7.   **Use of Technology.** Having scriptures and lyrics displayed on a projector screen, recorded sermons on CD, DVD and other forms of technology, aids us in learning the Word of God easier. Hence, it changes our thinking.

These are only a few things that are in your church that effect the way you think. Of course, your greatest influence should be the Word of God. However, it is safe to say that church attendance plays an important role in changing the way you think.

15. CHURCH ATTENDANCE CAUSES YOU TO FLOURISH WITH FAVOR

It's time for church members to flourish. God has a strategy for you to flourish. We see His plan in Psalms 92:12-15:

> The righteous shall flourish like the palm tree: he shall grow like a cedar in Lebanon. **13** Those that be planted in the house of the Lord shall flourish in the courts of our God. **14** They shall still bring forth fruit in old age; they shall be fat and flourishing; **15** To shew that the Lord *is* upright: *he is* my rock, and *there is* no unrighteousness in him.

When we plant ourselves in the house of the Lord, we experience favor and favor causes our lives to flourish. He says we will bring forth fruit in old age. That means that we'll still be able to serve the Lord and do good works in our old age. We can still be productive when we get old. He also said, the righteous shall be fat and flourishing. Don't get scared. It doesn't mean fat in body weight. Fat means lucrative, rich and fertile in the Strong's Concordance. The key to being lucrative, rich and fertile is attending church. We should be running to the church for all the rich, wonderful benefits that it causes to be produced in us.

CONGREGATIONAL FAVOR

Notice that God will make you lucrative, rich and fertile to show the world that He is upright. He is your rock and there is no unrighteousness in Him. Church attendance makes the difference in your life.

PROFESSIONAL CHURCH VISITORS

Today, people are professional church visitors. They go to church but never become a member of a local church. They are church squatters. They don't have any ownership in anything that the Lord has. They never officially help build anything. They never have an official pastor. It's kind of like a live-in girlfriend or boyfriend. You can call them your fiancé or your spouse, but it's not official. You have the ability to have sex, but it is not officially recognized by God as holy until you are married.

Professional Church Visitors are not official in God's eyes. They attend and might even give an offering but they are not receiving the benefits because they will not do it God's way. They believe that as long as they show-up sometimes they are alright. It's more than showing up. It's entering into covenant so you can grow. It's time to quit going to church only on first and third or second and fourth Sundays. Start attending every service so you can get the full benefits of Church attendance. Now that you understand the benefits of church attendance, let's take a look at the benefits of participating in church.

Chapter 3

The Benefits of Participating in Church

. . . .

> If any man serve me, let him follow me;
> and where I am, there shall also my
> servant be: if any man serve me, him will
> *my* Father honour. John 12:26

The church is a training ground for the people of God. When you participate in the church, you develop skills and abilities that are transferable to the world. The Lord gave skills to Bezaleel and Aholiab in Exodus 31:1-11 which they were able to use for the house of God and in the professional sector. He did the same for Zerubbabel and Joshua in the book of Haggai 1:13-15. When you serve the Lord, He can anoint you with favor so you can do great things in society.

In Job 36:11-12, we read, *"If they obey and serve him, they shall spend their days in prosperity, and their years in pleasures. But if they obey not, they shall perish by the sword, and they shall die without knowledge."*

The key is to serve. You cannot be considered obedient if you do not serve. When a person serves, they will have favor. Notice it says the servant will spend their days in prosperity and their years in pleasure. That's favor because of participation. The servant is the person who is working in the church. This includes everyone from the parking lot attendant, bus drivers, cleaning crew members, greeters, ushers, planning teams and all other roles in the church. This favor means that you will not have to depend on your résumé, degree or any other thing to make you prosperous. Your serving in the church will be the ultimate key to your success in this world.

In today's church, everyone wants to be paid for their service, especially musicians. God gave musicians talents and gifs. It is a shame that He has to buy it back from them in order to use it. They are no different than an usher, children's church worker, cleaning team member or any other position. They should serve and look for their rewards from God.

There are seven benefits you receive from participating in your church. I am going to show you each one. Every scriptural benefit will be associated exclusively with serving in the church, so you will see the word "servant" used in each scripture. That means these benefits only apply to those who serve in the

Lord's church. They are exclusive. If you have never served in the church, you are missing these benefits.

In earlier chapters, I explained that favor is found when you attend church. Participating in your church is another way you find this favor. These seven benefits only come to those who get involved in church. No involvement, no favor! Because of these benefits, the devil puts up such a strategic fight against people to stop them from serving in church. Take a look at these benefits of participation:

1. GOD WARNS AND REWARDS PEOPLE WHO SERVE IN CHURCH

> The law of the Lord *is* perfect, converting the soul: the testimony of the Lord *is* sure, making wise the simple. The statutes of the Lord *are* right, rejoicing the heart: the commandment of the Lord *is* pure, enlightening the eyes. The fear of the Lord *is* clean, enduring for ever: the judgments of the Lord *are* true *and* righteous altogether. More to be desired *are they* than gold, yea, than much fine gold: sweeter also than honey and the honeycomb. Moreover by them is thy servant warned: *and* in keeping of them *there* *is* great reward. Who can understand *his* errors? cleanse thou me

from secret *faults*. Keep back thy servant also from presumptuous *sins*; let them not have dominion over me: then shall I be upright, and I shall be innocent from the great transgression. Let the words of my mouth, and the meditation of my heart, be acceptable in thy sight, O Lord, my strength, and my redeemer. Psalms 19:7-14 .

Notice verse 11 says, "Moreover by them is thy servant warned..." When you are a servant, you are important to God's business in the earth. That's not to say all of His children are not important. Nevertheless, kingdom business must continue and God's servants get preference. Because you are preferred by God, He will warn you about things to come. He will show you things to come. He will warn you about accidents, people to avoid, upcoming financial problems and other things that might take you away from serving in His kingdom.

Looking further into verse 11 we find these words, "...and in keeping of them there is great reward." Notice that there is a "great reward" for the servant. I call this the "servant's reward". The servant's reward means that God is going to be responsible for compensating you for all your labors in His church. Many people look for some form of monetary payment for their deeds in the house of God. Instead, they should look for God to reward them. We see this mainly among church musicians. Many of them will not minister in music unless they get paid by the church.

A church musician is a servant in the church just like the ushers, the cleaning team, the greeters and everyone else who serves. He is no more deserving of financial reward than any other area of the ministry. In fact, there are teams in every church that put in longer hours, work harder or perform more overwhelming tasks than the musicians. The pastors have done a disservice to the kingdom of God by trying to grow their churches through music, instead of teaching the Word of God. Even if music grew the church, the lack of proper foundation will cause it to fall. Musicians, however, are subject to the same scriptures as all who work in the church. They should get a job, serve in the church, and look for their reward from God. Eventually, their musical skills coupled with faithfulness, can become a legitimate full time job at the church.

When you begin to serve in your local church, you are going to become a valuable part of God's team of spiritual employees. God is going to show you favor by warning you and rewarding you. This is a great benefit and it makes serving worthwhile all by itself. However, there are even more reasons why you should serve in your local church.

2. PEOPLE WHO SERVE IN THE CHURCH LIVE THE REDEEMED LIFE

God allows us to live a redeemed life when we serve in His church. In Psalms 34:22, we read the following, *"The Lord redeemeth the soul of his servants: and none of them that trust in him shall be desolate."* Generically, the word "redeemed" means "paid for by God". God has already paid for us as the Apostle Paul explained in 1 Corinthians 6:20, *"For ye are bought with a price: therefore glorify God in your body, and in your spirit, which are God's."* So the redeemed life is, "The life where everything I need is paid for by God."

To realize this benefit, all you need to do is participate in church. This benefit is like having an employee discount. When you work at a company, sometimes they give you a discount or even some free merchandise. Just like companies that offer employee discounts, God can give favor to His servants so they can have a discount or free merchandise. God does this so his children don't go without while they are taking care of His work.

My wife and I were in a restaurant and when we asked for the check, the attendant said that a person at another table had already paid the check for us. We did not know them and they did not know us. God placed it on their heart to take care of His servants. This is a benefit of the redeemed life.

Notice that the scripture says, "...and none of them that trust in him shall be desolate." When we serve in the church, we will not be without. A person who serves will always have someone to serve and somewhere to serve. Because that person serves, God will make sure they have a job, food, shelter and clothing. They will not be deserted by God nor left stranded in negative circumstances.

Remember this; you will never miss-out on any good thing as long as you serve the Lord. You will not have to worry about your bills if you serve in the Lord's house. You will never have to concern yourself about food when you serve in the church. Find a place to serve so you can enjoy the redeemed life.

3. GOD TAKES PLEASURE IN THE PROSPERITY OF HIS SERVANTS

Everyone wants to prosper and today we have an abundance of revelation on the subject of prosperity. Unfortunately, we do not have an abundance of prosperous Christians. This is due to a lack of understanding of the Word of God. Look at Psalms 35:27 with me.

Let them shout for joy, and be glad, that favour my righteous cause: yea, let them say continually, Let the Lord be magnified, which hath pleasure in the prosperity of his servant.

This is a favorite scripture among Christians, but there is one very important stipulation: You must be a servant. Prosperity in this scripture is reserved for those who serve God. No Service, No Prosperity! He did not say, "God take pleasure in the prosperity of His *children*." That would include everyone whether they served or not. Instead, it is limited to "servants". You will find favor to prosper when you start to participate at church.

Notice that the Psalm says, "God takes pleasure". When Christians get involved in church, God takes pleasure in them; and when God is happy, everybody is happy. When He is happy with His servant, He will be happy about prospering and blessing him. Your prosperity will cover every area of your life. It will cover your home, family, education, finances, church and anything that affects you being blessed. God takes pleasure in those who participate in his church.

4. GOD PROMISES TO BLESS THE CHILDREN OF THE SERVANTS

You are not the only beneficiary from your service in church. Your children can benefit from your service as well. In Psalms 102:27-28 we read, "But thou *art* the same, and thy years shall have no end. 28 The children of thy servants shall continue, and their seed shall be established before thee."

Once again, more favor attached to the "servant". This time it affects our children. He says the children of the servants shall "continue." This means they shall dwell safely, be blessed and prosperous. When you serve, your children have a right to be blessed beyond failure, hurt and anything that causes them to lose in life. To dwell safely also means long life. That means they will be around because God will keep them safe.

He also promised that their seed (your grandchildren) will be established. What a promise! Your service in the house of the Lord reaches all the way to your grandchildren. They will be established before you. I also have to point out that it indicates you will see this. That means long life for you. Even when you see one of your children going the wrong way, you can stand on the fact that you are a servant and God made a promise to you that they will be blessed.

When we begin to make it a priority to serve God, we can expect to see the blessing on our children and grandchildren. Here is another scripture I want you to look at. Psalms 69:35-36 says, *"For God will save Zion, and will build the cities of Judah: that they may dwell there, and have it in possession. 36 The seed also of his servants shall inherit it: and they that love his name shall dwell therein. Zion is metaphorically the church."* When you serve, your children see it and they begin to develop a servant's spirit in them as well. They inherit your sprit of leadership. They develop a spirit of excellence by watching how you serve. This ensures they will serve in the church one day, walk in congregational favor and see the blessing on their children and grandchildren.

How you serve is going to affect them as well. If they see you are faithful, they will respect the importance of faithfulness. If they see you are half-stepping, showing-up late, missing church and sowing a bunch of B.S. (Bad Seed) they will inherit those wicked ways as well. So serve and serve well. As a result, you will see your children and grandchildren become established and dwell safely in long life.

5. GOD EXALTS HIS SERVANTS

God wants to elevate and promote His servants through congregational favor. Your qualification for promotion is not your résumé or your degree. Your lack of qualification is not your past failures or your lack of skills or even your criminal record. To be promoted, you only need congregational favor. To walk in congregational favor for promotion you need two things:

1. Humility by Serving; and,
2. Submission through Service

HUMILITY BY SERVING

Humble people can expect to be promoted by God. Humility is not an act or display of softness or a special syntax. Humility is service. Actually, the key to promotion is serving others. The place where we serve others is in the church. When we serve others in the local church, we are openly demonstrating our humility to God and to man. In Matt 23:11-12, Jesus shares the following words:

> But he that is greatest among you shall be your servant. And whosoever shall exalt himself shall be abased; and he that shall humble himself shall be exalted."

Serving others in church is one true sign of humility. Many people have trouble serving because it requires you to be flexible. This, however, is what Jesus refers to as humility. True humility is serving others because it requires submission, obedience, paying attention to their needs, suffering a wrong, walking in love and so much more. These are the characteristics God looks for when exalting someone. Therefore, we could read this scripture like this:

> "But he that is greatest among you shall be your servant [demonstrating humility to God by serving your needs in the church]. And whosoever shall exalt himself [by

deeming himself too good to serve your needs in church] shall be abased; and he that shall humble himself [demonstrating humility to God by serving your needs in the church] shall be exalted."

SUBMISSION THROUGH SERVICE

The second element necessary to be promoted is "submission". Peter uses the principle of submission when talking to church members in 1 Peter 5:5-6.

Yea, all *of you* be subject one to another, and be clothed with humility: for God resisteth the proud, and giveth grace to the humble. Humble yourselves therefore under the mighty hand of God, that he may exalt you in due time:

He admonishes everyone to be subject to one another. Being subject to someone means being submitted. In this scripture, it also implies serving in the church because Peter is speaking to elders of the church as stated in the first verse. You cannot be submitted without service – it is impossible. Because Peter is speaking to church members, he desires that everyone be "submitted servants" in the church. Therefore, submitting and serving in the church is a good sign of humility.

Peter then says they should be clothed with humility. Now we can understand that he means clothed with humility by serving and submitted through service. If a person is not willing to submit and serve, it's obvious they are not humble. There is no revelation necessary to figure this out.

Jesus and Peter both connect promotion and higher standards of living to this kind of humility. The word "Exalt" means to "elevate" and to "lift up". Jesus said, *"and he that shall humble himself shall be exalted [elevated and lifted up]."* Peter explained, *"God resisteth the proud, and giveth grace to the humble. Humble yourselves therefore under the mighty hand of God, that he may exalt [elevate and lift up] you in due time."* When a person is humble, they will have the grace of God on their life. When we serve with a humble, submitted attitude we are qualified for the favor of God to come on our lives. We can then expect God to elevate us and lift us up to higher standards of living.

God does not have a problem with you becoming successful. When you have served in the church, He has no problem giving you an idea, anointing you for business or blessing your product. God promotes those who serve. When you serve in the church you will notice a correlation between your service and your status in life. Participate in church and watch God elevate you.

6. GOD GIVES PRIORITY TO THE PRAYERS OF HIS SERVANTS

God hears the prayers of the righteous. Just like a good businessman, the needs of His spiritual employees can take precedent. Our service to the Lord is like a company's name badge. In a company with thousands of employees, the CEO may not know every person's name. When an employee approaches him wearing his company issued name badge, he will give credence to that person simply because of the badge. A servant in the local church has this kind of status with God. He gives precedence to those who serve him.

We see Jesus giving precedent to the needs of His team of disciples. In Luke 4:38-39 we see Jesus healing Peter's mother-in-law so she could serve. *"And he arose out of the synagogue, and entered into Simon's house. And Simon's wife's mother was taken with a great fever; and they besought him for her. And he stood over her, and rebuked the fever; and it left her: and immediately she arose and ministered unto them."*

Here is another example of Jesus, giving precedence to a servant. Jesus healed the servant of a certain high ranking soldier. The reason He honored the request is found in the following verses of scripture:

> And a certain centurion's servant, who was dear unto him, was sick, and ready to die. 3 And when he heard of Jesus, he sent

unto him the elders of the Jews, beseeching him that he would come and heal his servant. 4 And when they came to Jesus, they besought him instantly, saying, That he was worthy for whom he should do this: 5 For he loveth our nation, and he hath built us a synagogue. Luke 7:2-5

Jesus honored this request for a person who was not Jewish and not in covenant with Him because he served the church by building a synagogue for the Jewish people. This is the same as building a church. This made him a spiritual employee and gave him credence with Jesus. Jesus healed his servant as a result.

During the time of Jesus' ministry, you never read in the Bible about any of his disciples suffering lack or going without. This is because while they served the Lord, the Lord took care of their needs. Jesus wants to take care of your needs. All you need to do is pray and He will honor your prayers and give credence to the importance of your service in His Church.

Your service in Church is very important to God. He is well aware that the business of meeting spiritual needs must continue. If you have unmet needs, it can and will hinder your work. Thus, God has a desire to meet your needs when you pray.

Look at this example in Psalms 143:12 of a prayer based solely on David's status of being a servant:

> And of thy mercy cut off mine enemies,
> and destroy all them that afflict my soul:
> for I *am* thy servant.

This dialog with God was not based on righteousness, character or anything other than "I am thy servant". David understood that God would honor his status. Someone might say, "Well God hears us because we are righteous" or "God hears us because of our right to use the Name of Jesus." Both statements are true; however, I believe that if two born-again believers talk to God – one a servant and another person who does not serve, the servant has an extra incentive to be heard. It doesn't make the servant better than the non-servant. It gives his situation a higher priority based on servanthood. We see this principle again in Psalms 119:124-125:

> Deal with thy servant according unto thy
> mercy, and teach me thy statutes. I *am* thy
> servant; give me understanding, that I
> may know thy testimonies.

Notice again that this prayer is prefaced with "I am thy servant". This request for mercy, teaching and understanding is definitely for a servant to acquire before a non-servant. He is going to need those essential tools to carryout the duties of the ministry.

God gives favor to those who serve by giving priority to their prayers. Hezekiah was one of the greatest servants of the Lord. He served the Lord by restoring righteousness to the land and caused the Levites to sanctify the house of the Lord. The Bible says there was never a king like him before or after him (2 Kings 18:5). In his later years, the Lord told him through the Prophet Isaiah, he was going to die of a sickness. Nevertheless, Hezekiah prayed from his position as a servant. Here is his prayer in Isaiah 38:2-3:

> Then Hezekiah turned his face toward the wall, and prayed unto the Lord, **3** And said, Remember now, O Lord, I beseech thee, how I have walked before thee in truth and with a perfect heart, and have done *that which is* good in thy sight. And Hezekiah wept sore.

He identified that he had served the Lord with a perfect heart. Hezekiah did not ask the Lord to heal him simply because he was the king, nor did he ask the Lord to heal him because he was better than the others. He reminded the Lord of his servant status and God heard his prayer based on that. As a result, the Lord healed him and added fifteen additional years to his life.

When you serve in the church, you will have status with God that enhances your righteousness with righteous actions. Because of this status, God will honor your prayer by giving you priority. That's favor.

> **10 Reasons People Do Not Serve in Church**
> 1. They Don't Want to Make a Commitment.
> 2. They Don't Understand the Blessing of Service.
> 3. They are Embarrassed to use their gift.
> 4. They Don't Feel Important.
> 5. They Feel Unworthy.
> 6. They Want to Be Paid to Serve.
> 7. They Don't Share the Same Style.
> 8. They Feel Too Talented to Serve.
> 9. They Become Weary.
> 10. They Don't know that they are Working with and for God.

7. SERVANTS ARE ANOINTED BY GOD

There will never be a greater favor in your life than the anointing of God. When God anoints you, it's because He has an assignment for you. Your anointing says that He trusts you. When you receive an assignment from God, it implies that you are going to be around to fulfill it. Thus, you can be assured, you are not going to die. God would not assign you something that you can not complete. In Psalms 89:19-27, we read the following:

> **19** Then thou spakest in vision to thy holy one, and saidst, I have laid help upon *one that is* mighty; I have exalted *one* chosen

out of the people. **20** I have found David my servant; with my holy oil have I anointed him: **21** With whom my hand shall be established: mine arm also shall strengthen him. **22** The enemy shall not exact upon him; nor the son of wickedness afflict him. **23** And I will beat down his foes before his face, and plague them that hate him. **24** But my faithfulness and my mercy *shall be* with him: and in my name shall his horn be exalted. **25** I will set his hand also in the sea, and his right hand in the rivers. **26** He shall cry unto me, Thou *art* my father, my God, and the rock of my salvation. **27** Also I will make him *my* firstborn, higher than the kings of the earth.

We see that God anoints David to do His work. The anointing of God made him a vessel carrying the burden removing, yoke destroying, forever abiding, and all knowing power of God on his life. Because David was anointed by God, he was equipped for success. God promised several things for David. Here is a list of some of the things we find in these verses:

1. David would have the hand of God, verse 21

2. David would have the Strength of God, verse 21
3. The enemy would not do violence to him, verse 22
4. The wicked would not afflict him, verse 22
5. God would beat his enemies for him, verse 23
6. God would plague his haters, verse 23
7. God would be faithful and merciful to him, verse 24
8. He would have great power and prosperity, verse 24
9. He would have power in the seas and rivers, verse 25
10. God would answer his prayers, verse 26

All of these favors were given to David because God anointed him to fulfill his assignment. When you serve in the church, God will anoint you as well. You can expect God to do these sorts of things in your life when you serve. There is always great favor for great servants.

Now that you know the benefits of participating in church, make sure you become involved so you can participate in the rewards God has for your life. In the next chapter, we will take a look at another important aspect of Congregational Favor – The Benefits of Defending Your Church.

Chapter 4

The Benefits of Defending Your Church

. . . .

Every Church Must Be Defended

God built everything with a defense mechanism. We humans, have an immune system to protect us from diseases. Animals and insects have defenses to help them avoid or to keep predators at bay. The earth has the atmosphere that causes objects like meteors to burn up before destroying the earth. Oceans, rivers, and streams have movement to keep them from developing diseases. Christians have angels to protect them against evil and plagues (Psalm 91).

As you can see, it's only natural to have a defense. We put alarms on our cars and homes. We place our money in banks and safes. America's constitution says we have the right to bear arms. Everything God has created has a defense, so why doesn't the church? Your church needs a defense against predators and attackers.

CONGREGATIONAL FAVOR

It is not a sin to defend your church. The greater sin is to allow someone to destroy it.

I have two questions for you and I have taken the guesswork out by providing you with the correct answers. Here they are:

> *Question Number 1: Would you allow a brick to be thrown through your car window if you could prevent it?* **Answer:** *No. You have paid too much money for your car to allow someone to damage it.*
>
> *Question Number 2: Would you allow someone to break into your home and steal everything you worked so hard to acquire if you could avoid it?* **Answer:** *No. You worked too hard for all those things and some of them cannot be replaced.*

If you answered no to the above two question, and I hope you did, then why would you allow someone to destroy your church? Think about it like this, you have been paying your tithes from the same hard earned money you purchased your car and home with. You have been giving offerings and sowing seed from the same hard earned money. You have irreplaceable memories that you and your family have built over the years at your church. Your church is just as valuable, if not more valuable, than the car, home and precious memories. In most cases, it was the teaching you received at your church that helped you get the car, buy the home, and save your family so you could create those memories. You should take extra pride and care to assure your church is protected and well cared for.

Just like you have an alarm on your car and your home, every member must become an alarm mechanism against the various forms of destructive church behavior. Even Jesus let us know about our responsibility to protect His church. Look at what He said, *"Verily, verily, I say unto you, He that entereth not by the door into the sheepfold, but climbeth up some other way, the same is a thief and a robber"(John 10:1). "The thief cometh not, but for to steal, and to kill, and to destroy..." (John 10:10). "But know this, that if the goodman of the house had known in what watch the thief would come, he would have watched, and would not have suffered his house to be broken up." (Matthew 24:43).*

Paul also was a good example of a defender of the church. He said in Philippians 1:17, *"...I am set for the defence of the gospel."* Look at the following scriptures and see how Paul defended the church where Timothy was the pastor.

> Do thy diligence to come shortly unto me: **10** For Demas hath forsaken me, having loved this present world, and is departed unto Thessalonica; Crescens to Galatia, Titus unto Dalmatia. **11** Only Luke is with me. Take Mark, and bring him with thee:

for he is profitable to me for the ministry.
2 Timothy 4:9-11.

Alexander the coppersmith did me much evil: the Lord reward him according to his works: **15** Of whom be thou ware also; for he hath greatly withstood our words. 2 Tim 4:14-15.

Notice that Paul identified Demas had forsaken him. The main characteristic of Demas was his love for this world. People who come into your church with the spirit that Demas has will be very worldly. They are into things, toys and temptation. They don't resist anything the world has to offer. They will eventually leave for their worldly things after they have hurt people. They hurt people by using them for their own pleasures without making any commitments in return. Paul made Timothy aware of Demas just in case Demas decided to become a harmful threat to Timothy's church.

He specifically reported Alexander so that the evil he caused Paul would not be perpetrated against Timothy. He identified Alexander as a coppersmith to expose that he was a businessman. Many times, people use their businesses to destroy the church. They use the church to build a clientele and then persuade their clients to leave the church. Defending your church might require you to address a person's conduct directly or report it to the pastor or leadership. Remember, God created everything with a defense system. Let's look at another scripture:

> I wrote unto the church: but Diotrephes, who loveth to have the preeminence among them, receiveth us not. 10 Wherefore, if I come, I will remember his deeds which he doeth, prating against us with malicious words: and not content therewith, neither doth he himself receive the brethren, and forbiddeth them that would, and casteth *them* out of the church. 11 Beloved, follow not that which is evil, but that which is good. He that doeth good is of God: but he that doeth evil hath not seen God. 3 John 1:9-11.

This time the Apostle John makes it clear by identifying Diotrephes and his actions against God's people. Every church is going to have an Alexander, Demas or a Diotrephes to deal with every now and then. It's important that you know how to identify them so you can stop them before they destroy God's work. So far we looked at Alexander and Demas. Let's take a look at the characteristics of Diotrephes:

- **He Loved to have the Preeminence.** He wanted to be most important. He wanted to be first. He wanted to be the best. People who desire this feel threatened when they are around other leaders. They work to get themselves to appear to be better than others. They always reference how good it was at their last church.

- **He did not Receive John.** John noticed the Diotrephes was not receiving from him. People who are destructive to a church do not receive from the pastors of the church. They will not support the events the pastors put in place to benefit the members. For an example, they will avoid the women's fellowship if the pastors' wife teaches it. They give the impression that these events won't benefit them or they know more than the pastor(s).
- **He was Prating.** When John was not around, he kept babbling and berating John verbally using malicious words. He was a gossiper and he attempted to make John look small in the eyes of the people. There will be people who will try to make the pastors and his leadership team feel small so they themselves can seem important.
- **He used Malicious Words.** Malicious means hurtful. Diotrephes used hurtful words. The words of people like Diotrephes are hurtful to the pastors, leadership and to the church at large. If words don't build up the church, they are hurtful. If they point out the negatives of the church, they are hurtful. Malicious people will praise their former pastors and craftily castigate their current pastors and church.
- **He kept Forbidding People from Coming into the Church.** People like Diotrephes work very hard to meet the new people and introduce them to the

negative situations regarding the church. These distractions prevent visitors and guests from joining the church. They have a repelling spirit. The faster they are dealt with, the quicker your church can grow. When our church had a Diotrephes in it, it would not grow. When they left, the church grew immediately.

- **He Kicked People out of the Church.** Their constant negative actions and behavior cause people to leave. Some of them will personally invite your members to other people's fellowships with the intent of helping them find a place "they feel" would be better. Instead of allowing them to kick others out of the church, they need to be kicked out of the church. I personally tried to dismiss someone from our church, but she decided she wanted to stay. I concluded she wanted to leave on her own terms. She wanted to have the preeminence.

Notice that John said, *"Wherefore, if I come, I will remember his deeds which he doeth."* John was not scared to deal with Diotrephes. In verse 9, John made it perfectly clear that if he comes, he will deal with him. You cannot sit idly by and let Demas, Alexander and Diotrephes determine the destiny of your church.

EMPOWER LEADERS TO DEAL WITH A.D.D.

A.D.D. stands for Attention Deficit Disorder. It also means, Alexander, Demas and Diotrephes which is a church version of Attention Deficit Disorder. It will make your members lose the ability to focus their attention on the Word and the positive things that your church is doing. One day, one of our A.D.D. members began to go viral and started attempting to spread her disorder with our leaders. She began to cleverly speak to leaders individually to get them to identify the negative situations in our church. The leaders were completely empowered to shutdown the nonsense and they did. The leaders began to exclude her from the areas of ministry in which she worked. She saw that her A.D.D. did not fit well in our church culture and eventually her and her family left the church.

How to Identify a Viral Person in Your Church
1. They Attempt to Make the Pastor Look incompetent
2. They Stop Attending Services Regularly
3. They Begin Sitting in the Back of the Church
4. They Share their Differences of Opinion between the Leadership of the church.
5. They Offer their "Professional Opinion" as the ultimate Solution to the church's progress
6. They Avoid Talking to Leadership who don't tolerate viral behavior
7. They Start Looking For Other Churches Openly
8. They tell people that the Spirit of God is not Moving Here any Longer

EVERY CHURCH SHOULD HAVE A GOSSIP POLICY

There are many reasons why people leave a church. Some reasons are good and some are bad. My heart goes out to those faithful members and pastors who have suffered "exit abuse" by someone who decided to leave a church inappropriately. My heart also goes out to those faithful members and pastors who have or are suffering through someone who really should leave, but has decided to stay and spread a bunch of B.S. (Bad Seed) around the church. And then, there is the person who is totally unaware of the harm they're causing. They are simply sharing what they heard and not really considering the harm it's causing. Finally, there's the person who listens to all the latest church news and either enjoys hearing it, or doesn't know how to deal with it. I heard it said that the number one reason a person leaves a church is because of gossip. The number two reason is the failure of the pastor to deal with the gossip.

As a good member, I encourage you to speak to your church leadership regarding the development of a gossip policy. Every church must have a gossip policy to minimize and even eliminate the problems that gossip causes in a church. A gossip policy is your first line of defense against those who are experts at using their tongue to manipulate the decisions of others. When implemented properly, this policy will make everyone feel emotionally safe in your church. It will stop the gossip bullies from attacking the innocent members of your church. Most of all, it will potentially eliminate the number one and number two reasons why people leave your church. Once we put our gossip policy in place, we've only had to use it one time.

We call it a gossip policy for short, but it includes other sins of the mouth that negatively affect members and the church overall. You might as well prepare and arm your church members to deal with everything the devil brings against you before it happens. After your church has decided to put your policy in place, make sure it covers the following topics:

1. Gossip.
2. Strife.
3. Backbiting.
4. Meddling.
5. Discord.
6. Murmuring and Complaining.
7. Spiritual Gossip. Spreading the prayer requests and needs of other around the church without their permission.
8. How gossip, strife, backbiting, meddling etc. will be handled
9. Who can enforce the policy?
10. The penalty for violating the gossip policy.

The final step in creating your gossip policy is to make sure that everyone knows the policy. We introduced our policy to the following groups in this order:

1. **Leadership.** Don't assume they know the policy. They are usually the first people to gossip.
2. **Congregation.** As the pastor, I taught it from the pulpit to the members so they could hear it from me. I also include it in various messages from time to time. If it's the number on reason people leave your church, shouldn't it be your number one topic from time to time?
3. **New Members Courses.** This must be a staple in your new members' course. Every member must hear it, see it and sign it.
4. **Ministry of Helps Training and Orientation Courses.** Make sure it's reiterated to anyone receiving training to work on your team(s). When people start working with others, they forget about policies depending on their emotional state for that day.

HOW TO HELP DEFEND YOUR CHURCH

It's impossible to tell you everything you need to know to defend your church. There are so many circumstances that your church will face over the years. However, once you get the concepts the rest will come to you naturally and by the knowledge of the Word of God and the power of the Holy Spirit. You already understand the need for a gossip policy, so here are a few other tips to get you started.

1. **Pray for Your Pastors and Your Church.** God hears the prayer of church members when their church is dealing with negative people.

2. **Know Your Church Vision.** Most people who attack churches don't understand the church's vision. Likewise, most victims of attacks don't know the vision of their church. When you know the vision of your church, you will be qualified to deal with negative people.

3. **Leadership Training and Empowerment.** If your church does not have leadership training, ask your pastor if he would consider implementing this kind of course. Leaders must be empowered against Alexander, Demas and Diotrephes when they decide to go viral. A leader must know these things.to be empowered:

  a. Leaders Must Know The Gossip Policy. Leaders cannot be empowered without knowledge of how the policy works and how to implement it.

b. Leaders Must Know They Have the Pastor's Ear. Leaders cannot be afraid or intimidated to come to the pastor with names. The pastor must require names.

c. Leaders Must Know the Pastor is Free from Impartiality. The leader must not fear the pastor will be impartial because of the pastor's extended family (Brother, Cousin, Mother, etc). Family members can have A.D.D also.

d. Leaders Must Know How to Shut A.D.D. Down. Every leader must know how to stop viral members before they do damage. They must know the proper procedure and process for releasing them from working on their teams.

4. **Be Direct with Negative People.** You must make it a point to speak very direct with a negative person. Limit their chances to discuss negative communication again. This will begin to establish boundaries again. Don't be afraid. When you are right, God is on your side. Remember what John said after he addressed the issue with Diotrephes, "Beloved, follow not that which is evil, but that which is good. He that doeth good is of God: but he that doeth evil hath not seen God."

5. **Expose Negative People before they get too Viral.** When you are constantly impacted by an A.D.D. member, take their negative feedback to the other leaders at the next meeting. Just report the facts. Don't add anything to it. Do not add your opinion or your feelings. Just report the facts.

6. **Allow the Leaders to Get on the Same Page Regarding Negative People.** Every church should have a watch list for negative members. Each leader should have the same response when they are impacted. This is scriptural. In 1 Corinthians 1:10-11, Paul addresses a negative situation that had gone viral by stating, *"Now I beseech you, brethren, by the name of our Lord Jesus Christ, that ye all speak the same thing, and that there be no divisions among you; but that ye be perfectly joined together in the same mind and in the same judgment. 11 For it hath been declared unto me of you, my brethren, by them which are of the house of Chloe, that there are contentions among you."* Paul said to "speak the same thing" when dealing with negative people. When they come to one leader, the answer should be the same as if they went to the pastor or another leader. When a leader says something different, they are probably viral already.

7. **Don't Over Do It.** There will always be negative people in the church. You don't want your church to

become a place where everyone is like the police. That's why the Leaders need to be empowered to deal with the issue directly so it can be resolved. Always correct people with the hope and expectation that they will repent and change their ways. This doesn't always happen, but it should be your ambition.

8. **Let Them Go**. If the person leaves the church, let them go. If it's your family and they leave, let them go. If you try to keep them around, they will feel empowered by your need for them. Don't do an exit interview with them to find out why they are leaving. They are leaving because they need to leave before the lives of more people get destroyed or impacted. Support your pastor when he has to address these kinds of issues in the church, even if it's your family.

9. **Ask the Negative Person if they Have Permission to Be that Negative**. When people are involved in gossip, ask them if they have permission from the person they're speaking about to share their information. When they say no, tell them to stop sharing with you or anyone else. Also, let them know they if you hear a report of them sharing the information, you will resort to bringing them before the church leadership.

10. **Offer the Negative Person an opportunity to sit down with a leader, church administrator or the Pastor.** If the person has a history of negative conduct and their conduct is impacting you, let that person know that you are taking it before the leaders of the church. 1 Thessalonians 5:14 Now we exhort you, brethren, warn them that are unruly....

11. **Do Not Communicate with Negative People.** This is an end to all strife, at least in your life. Viral people can only be viral if there is a receptor. It's just as much a sin to listen to negativity as it is to speak it. Don't allow your ears to become the slop buckets for everyone else's mess. 1 Corinthians 5:9-13 reads, *"I wrote unto you in an epistle not to company with fornicators: 10 Yet not altogether with the fornicators of this world, or with the covetous, or extortioners, or with idolaters; for then must ye needs go out of the world. 11 But now I have written unto you not to keep company, if any man that is called a brother be a fornicator, or covetous, or an idolater, or a railer, or a drunkard, or an extortioner; with such an one no not to eat. 12 For what have I to do to judge them also that are without? do not ye judge them that are within? 13 But them that are without God judgeth. Therefore put away from among yourselves that wicked person."*

12. **Ask Negative People to Leave.** If they are so unhappy at your church, tell them not to fight

against the powers that be – just leave. Tell them to leave before someone gets hurt. Usually when someone has gone viral and they're asked to leave, their response is, "God hasn't released me yet." Translated: I am not finished sowing my B.S. (Bad Seed) into the lives of others. Titus 3:10-11 reads, "*A man that is an heretic after the first and second admonition reject; 11 Knowing that he that is such is subverted, and sinneth, being condemned of himself.*" The word Heretic means "*a schismatic; a person who causes division*" according to the Strong's Concordance.

13. **Don't Investigate.** Don't lend credence to viral people by investigating. Your desire to investigate could be an enticement to sin. Anytime a person had negative conduct, unless they truly repent, they will have a justification for themselves. It doesn't make them right. Also remember, the spirit they operate in is adept at persuading people. Unclean spirits are transferrable. They are transferred by negative communication.

FAVOR FOR DEFENDING YOUR CHURCH

God does not want His church destroyed. When Saul was destroying the church, God intervened. God cares for His church and we should also. When we defend our church, we are defending the Gospel of Jesus Christ. In doing so, we obtain the favor of God as stated in

CONGREGATIONAL FAVOR

Philippians 1:7, "*... and in the defence and confirmation of the gospel, ye all are partakers of my grace.*" He is how we benefit from defending God's church:

1. WHEN WE DEFEND GOD'S CHURCH, GOD WILL DEFEND US

> Romans 16:17-20 (KJV) **17** Now I beseech you, brethren, mark them which cause divisions and offences contrary to the doctrine which ye have learned; and avoid them. **18** For they that are such serve not our Lord Jesus Christ, but their own belly; and by good words and fair speeches deceive the hearts of the simple. **19** For your obedience is come abroad unto all *men*. I am glad therefore on your behalf: but yet I would have you wise unto that which is good, and simple concerning evil. **20** And the God of peace shall bruise Satan under your feet shortly. The grace of our Lord Jesus Christ *be* with you. Amen.

The phrase "mark them" is the word "Skopeo" in the Greek according the Strong's Concordance. It means to take *aim* at (*spy*), consider, take heed or look at. God never intended for people who cause division and offenses to hinder His work. He wants us to intentionally watch them and even aim at stopping them. He said they do not serve the Lord when they do these things. No one ever serves the Lord by causing division.

When we decide to "mark them" we are choosing to protect our church. In doing so, Paul said *"the God of peace shall bruise satan under your feet shortly"*. The devil is your greatest enemy. When you defend God's church against negative people, God will defend you against satan and his strategies. Everything the devil wants to do to you, you have a defense for.

2. WHEN WE DEFEND OUR CHURCH THE LORD WILL GIVE US PEACE

> But ye, brethren, be not weary in well doing. 14 And if any man obey not our word by this epistle, note that man, and have no company with him, that he may be ashamed. 15 Yet count *him* not as an enemy, but admonish *him* as a brother. 16 Now the Lord of peace himself give you peace always by all means. The Lord *be* with you all. 2 Thessalonians 3:13-16

Peace comes to those who are defenders of their church. Notice that the Apostle Paul identifies a negative person as someone who does not obey the scriptures. He said we are not to have any company with him so that person will be ashamed. It's important that

CONGREGATIONAL FAVOR

a person who has wronged the church is ashamed of what he or she has done. This type of shame is healthy because it brings conviction. They will not feel ashamed if they are continuously welcomed by the members even though they have done bad things.

Just because they have wronged the church doesn't mean they should be treated as an enemy. Paul said to admonish them as a brother in the Lord. That means speak the truth to them. Share with them their mistakes. Don't pamper them as if they need to be consoled. Work to get them back on course. Many times we make the mistake of assuming that everyone who has done something wrong is an enemy. There are enemies to every church. However, people do make mistakes. A person who makes a mistake is still a brother in the Lord and need room to repent. Eventually, if the situation is handled properly, they will have a change in their heart and repent for the wrong they have done.

How do you identify an enemy to the church versus a person who has become disobedient? An enemy will continue to work against the church and will not accept admonishment from those who care. They never repent for what they have done. A brother in the Lord who wrongs the church will accept the admonishment. They repent for what they have done and they look for restoration.

Page | **98**

11 Reasons People Don't Defend Their Church
1. They are afraid.
2. The perpetrators are their family/friends
3. They are part of the problem
4. They enjoy listening to the issues
5. They are immature
6. They don't see the danger
7. They believe that God doesn't want them to intervene
8. They don't know that they will be blessed by defending their church
9. They were unaware it was going on
10. They thought it was the job of the Pastor
11. They are sympathetic to the perpetrators

Whenever you follow the steps that Paul prescribed in this chapter, you are now defending your church properly. In verse 16, Paul says, *"Now the Lord of peace himself give you peace always by all means. The Lord be with you all."* He is letting us know that we can expect two things when we defend our church:

1. **Peace.** The Lord Himself will give us peace always by all means. That means that no matter what we are going through, God will give us peace. No matter what it takes to make sure you have peace, He will do it. You will never have a shortage of peace. It will be available to you because you kept peace in Gods' church.

2. ***The Lord will be with you all.*** You will always have the presence of the Lord. In fact, He said "you all". That means the Lord will be with everyone who had a part of defending the church. When the Lord is with you in life, you will never have to worry about winning the battles that come your way.

Defending your church is not the responsibility of just one person. It's the responsibility of every member who loves their church and the Body of Christ. When we take time to defend our church, we can expect God to bless us with Congregational Favor. I trust this book has been a blessing to you and continues to be a resource for training Christians around the world. God bless you.

APPENDIX A

Prayer for Salvation

If you would like to accept Jesus as your personal Lord and Savior, pray this prayer:

Dear Heavenly Father,

I believe in the Lord Jesus Christ. I believe with my heart that He died for my sins. I believe with my heart that You raised Him from the dead. Jesus, I ask You to come into my heart and save me as You have promised in Your Word. I thank You for salvation in the Name of Jesus, Amen.

Prayer for Rededication

If you have backslidden and would like to return to Jesus, Pray this prayer:

Dear Heavenly Father,

I have sinned against You. I repent of my sin. You promised in your Word that if I confess my sins, You will forgive me and cleanse me from all unrighteousness. I ask for Your forgiveness right now in the Name of Jesus. Thank You for Your loving-kindness and tender mercies. I accept Your forgiveness today in the Name of Jesus, Amen.

APPENDIX B

Prayer for the Baptism of the Holy Spirit

If you are born-again and would like to receive the Baptism of the Holy Spirit, pray this prayer:

Dear Heavenly Father,

I accepted Jesus Christ as my Lord and Savior. You promised that you would pour Your Spirit out upon all flesh and allow your Spirit to live inside of man. I ask You to fill me with Your Holy Spirit with the evidence of speaking in tongues. I receive the Holy Spirit right now in the Name of Jesus, Amen.

Prayer for a Church Home

If you are born-again and would like to find the church God desires for you to join, pray this prayer:

Dear Heavenly Father,

Your word teaches that You set Your people in the church as it pleases You. I ask You to send me to a church that I can learn the Word of God, participate and become a faithful disciple of Yours. Please send me to a church that will please You. I thank You for my new church home now in the Name of Jesus, Amen.

APPENDIX C

Prayer for Healing

If you are sick in your body and would like to be healed, pray this prayer:

Dear Heavenly Father,

Many times in Your Word You provided healing for Your people. You also said that Jesus, **Himself took our infirmities, and bare *our* sicknesses (Matt 8:17)**. I believe that Jesus did this for me and all of His children. I also believe that You are able to heal any and all sickness and disease. Therefore, I ask You to heal me of _____ (name the sickness). I thank You for Your mercy in the Name of Jesus, Amen.

About the Author

Dr. Bryant Bell and his wife Dr. LySandra Bell are the Founders and Pastors of Enlightened Christian Center, a contemporary non-denominational church located in Marietta, GA. They founded the church in 1999 with no members and it has grown and become a very successful ministry reaching the world with the Gospel of Jesus Christ.

Dr. Bell also has a live Webcast that is streamed throughout the world. He also produces the Enlightened Living Broadcast, which can be viewed on demand 24 hours a day 7 days a week on the Internet at www.ecclive.org. Bryant Bell provides guidance and mentoring for many other pastors.

Dr. Bryant Bell has been married to Dr. LySandra since 1988. They have three children, Bryandra, Jeremy and Micaiah.